AMAZ BATS

AMAZ

BY KATE RIGGS

CREATIVE EDUCATION • CREATIVE PAPERBACKS

Published by Creative Education and
Creative Paperbacks
P.O. Box 227, Mankato, Minnesota 56002
Creative Education and Creative Paperbacks are
imprints of The Creative Company
www.thecreativecompany.us

Design by The Design Lab
Production by Angela Korte and Colin O'Dea
Art direction by Rita Marshall
Printed in the United States of America

Photographs by Alamy (AGAMI Photo Agency, National Geographic Image Collection, Rolf Nussbaumer), Dreamstime (Worldfoto), Getty Images (Theo Allofs/Corbis Documentary, DE AGOSTINI PICTURE LIBRARY, Hans Neleman, Jon Read/Moment, Dennis Stewart/500px, Carlton Ward/National Geographic Image Collection), iStockphoto (Martin Janča, KirsanovV, Mark Kostich, Y.Gurevich)

Library of Congress Cataloging-in-Publication Data
Names: Riggs, Kate, author.
Title: Bats / Kate Riggs.
Series: Amazing animals.
Includes bibliographical references and index.
Summary: This revised edition surveys key aspects of bats, describing the flying mammals' appearance, behaviors, and habitats. A folk tale explains why these creatures are nocturnal.
Identifiers: ISBN 978-1-64026-204-1 (hardcover) / ISBN 978-1-62832-767-0 (pbk) / ISBN 978-1-64000-329-3 (eBook)
This title has been submitted for CIP processing under LCCN 2019937906.

CCSS: RI.1.1, 2, 4, 5, 6, 7; RI.2.2, 5, 6, 7, 10; RI.3.1, 5, 7, 8; RF.1.1, 3, 4; RF.2.3, 4

First Edition HC 9 8 7 6 5 4 3 2 1
First Edition PBK 9 8 7 6 5 4 3 2 1

Table of Contents

Flying Mammals   4

Megabats and Microbats   8

Bat Pups   15

Nocturnal Flight   16

Flying Out   20

A Bat Tale   22

Read More   24

Websites   24

Index   24

Thin skin stretches between each finger to form strong, flexible wings.

Bats can be found all around the world. Most bats live in warm places. There are more than 1,200 kinds of bats. They are the only **mammals** that fly.

mammals animals that have hair or fur and feed their babies milk

All bats have two large wings and small feet. Their bodies are covered with soft fur. Some bats are yellow, gray, red, or even orange. But most are black or brown.

Tiny Honduran white bats sport fluffy, white fur.

The biggest bats are giant golden-crowned flying foxes. Their wings stretch more than five feet (1.5 m) across! Bumblebee bats are the smallest bats. They are only 1.2 inches (3 cm) long. They weigh less than a penny!

Flying foxes weigh fewer than three pounds (1.4 kg).

Microbats may hibernate in caves or crevices for six months.

The two groups of bats are megabats and microbats. Megabats live in warm places. Microbats like heat, too, but they can also live in cooler areas. Many **hibernate** when it gets too cold. Some **migrate** to warmer areas for winter.

hibernate spend the winter in one place, sleeping most of the time

migrate move from one area to another, especially regularly by the seasons

Megabats spread pollen and seeds, while microbats get rid of pests.

Megabats eat fruit. Some eat **nectar**, too. Microbats eat insects, frogs, and birds. Some even eat fish. The three kinds of vampire bats are microbats. They eat blood from animals.

nectar a sugary liquid made by plants

Flying fox pups stay with their mothers longer than other bat pups do.

Most mother bats have one **pup** each year. Newborn microbats are blind and hairless. Megabats are born with their eyes open. They have fur. Pups drink their mother's milk. They start flying when they are two to six weeks old.

pup a baby bat

Bat legs lock in place, allowing them to sleep without losing their grip.

Bats are nocturnal animals. This means that they sleep in the daytime and are awake at night. Bats **roost** upside down in trees or caves during the day. They fly around at night. This is when they find food.

roost come together with other bats to sleep or rest

Echolocation even tells microbats which direction prey is moving.

Megabats can see colors. This helps them find fruits that are ready to eat. Microbats find food through **echolocation** (*EK-oh-loh-KAY-shun*). This tells them when **prey** is close by. Then they swoop in and catch it.

echolocation finding things by sending out a sound and hearing the echoes that bounce back off the surroundings

prey animals that are killed and eaten by other animals

People can see bats in caves. Thousands of Mexican free-tailed bats live in Carlsbad Caverns National Park in New Mexico. Many people can see bats near their homes, too. It is exciting to see these winged mammals fly through the night!

Nearly 50 different kinds of bats can be found in the United States.

A Bat Tale

Long ago, the lion became king of the jungle. He told the bats to pick the group they belonged to. The bats said they were mammals. But the mammals said bats did not belong because they had wings. So the bats tried to join the birds. The birds said bats did not belong because they did not lay eggs. This is why bats only come out at night when other creatures are asleep.

Read More

Brown, Laaren. *Brilliant Bats*. New York: Scholastic, 2016.

Rissman, Rebecca. *Bats: Nocturnal Flyers*. Chicago: Heinemann Library, 2015.

Terp, Gail. *Bats*. North Mankato, Minn.: Black Rabbit Books, 2018.

Websites

Enchanted Learning: Bat Shape Book
https://www.enchantedlearning.com/subjects/mammals/bat/shapebook/
This site has printouts that can be made into a book about bats.

KidZone Animals: Bats
https://www.kidzone.ws/animals/bats/index.htm
Look at bat photos, read bat facts, and complete "batty" activities.

National Geographic Kids: Bat Myths Busted
https://kids.nationalgeographic.com/explore/nature/bat-myths-busted
Learn more about bats, including common misunderstandings.

Note: Every effort has been made to ensure that the websites listed above are suitable for children, that they have educational value, and that they contain no inappropriate material. However, because of the nature of the Internet, it is impossible to guarantee that these sites will remain active indefinitely or that their contents will not be altered.

Index

caves 16, 20
echolocation 19
feet 7
flying 4, 15, 16, 20
food 12, 15, 16, 19
fur 7, 15
megabats 8, 11, 12, 15, 19
microbats 8, 11, 12, 15, 19, 20
pups 15
sizes 8
trees 16
wings 7, 8, 22